St. ⟨ **P9-BJY-138** y

PowerKids Readers:

Bilingual Edition

My World of ANIMALS™

Edición Bilingüe

BEARS
OSOS

NATASHYA WILSON
TRADUCCIÓN AL ESPAÑOL:
NATHALIE BEULLENS

The Rosen Publishing Group's
PowerKids Press™ & **Editorial Buenas Letras**™
New York

1

For Dad, a.k.a. Père, happy birthday!

Published in 2004 by The Rosen Publishing Group, Inc.
29 East 21st Street, New York, NY 10010

First Edition

Book Design: Mike Donnellan
Illustration by Mike Donnellan

Photo Credits: Cover, pp. 11, 13, 19, 22 © CORBIS; pp. 5, 7, 9, 15 © Digital Vision Ltd.; p. 17 © AP/Wide World Photos; p. 21 © Scott Wm. Hanrahan/International Stock.

Library of Congress Cataloging-in-Publication Data

Wilson, Natashya.
 Bears = Osos / Natashya Wilson ; translated by Nathalie Beullens.– 1st ed.
  p. cm. – (My world of animals)
Summary: Provides an easy-to-read introduction to the life of bears and their habitat.
 ISBN 1-4042-7518-5 (lib. bdg.)
 1. Bears–Juvenile literature. [1. Bears. 2. Spanish language materials–Bilingual.]
I. Title: Osos. II. Title. III. Series.
 QL737.C27W57 2004
 599.78–dc21
                                                    2003008773

Manufactured in the United States of America

2

CONTENTS

CONTENIDO

This is a bear.

Este es un oso.

5

Bears roar. They have sharp teeth and big paws.

Los osos rugen. Tienen dientes muy filosos y patas grandes.

7

Some bears eat fish. They catch fish in rivers.

Algunos osos comen pescado que atrapan en los ríos.

Some bears live in the mountains. This is a grizzly bear.

Ciertos osos viven en las montañas. Este es un oso grizzly.

11

This is a polar bear. Polar bears live in very cold places. They walk on ice.

Este es un oso polar. Los osos polares viven en lugares muy fríos y caminan sobre el hielo.

13

This is a panda bear.
Panda bears live in forests and
eat plants.

Este es un oso panda.
Los pandas viven en los
bosques y comen plantas.

15

Some bears live in zoos and have toys. This bear has a ball.

Algunos osos viven en zoológicos y tienen juguetes. Este oso tiene una pelota.

Mother bears take care of their babies. A baby bear is called a cub.

Las mamás oso se ocupan de sus bebés. A un bebé oso se le llama cachorro.

18

19

This cub is watching its
mother swim. Bear cubs learn
from their mothers.

Este cachorro está mirando
cómo nada su mamá.
Los ositos aprenden todo de
sus mamás.

Words to Know
Palabras que debes saber

cub /
cachorro

fish /
pescado

mountains /
montañas

teeth /
dientes

Here are more books to read about bears/
Otros libros que puedes leer sobre osos:

In English/En inglés:
Black Bears
Brown Bears
Famous Bears
Panda Bears
Polar Bears
by Diana Star Helmer
Rosen Publishing

In Spanish/En español:
El oso (Bears)
by Claude Delafosse and Philippe Biard
Colección Mundo Maravilloso

Due to the changing nature of Internet links,
PowerKids Press has developed an online list of
Web sites related to the subject of this book. This
site is updated regularly. Please use this link to
access the list:

www.buenasletraslinks.com/myanim/oso/

Index

Índice

Words in English: 102   Palabras en español: 110

Note to Parents, Teachers, and Librarians
PowerKids Readers books *en español* are specially designed for emergent Hispanic readers and students learning Spanish in the United States. Simple stories and concepts are paired with photographs of real kids in real-life situations. Sentences are short and simple, employing a basic vocabulary of sight words, as well as new words that describe familiar things and places. With their engaging stories and vivid photo-illustrations, PowerKids *en español* gives children the opportunity to develop a love of reading and learning that they will carry with them throughout their lives.